Foreword

Whilst I believe you should consider seriously all the advice and insight that is given in this book, it is purposely written in a light hearted and observational manner. Therefore it is a guide as to what was and what now is possible.

Remember two things:

Etiquette, as defined by the Oxford English Dictionary is given as follows: Noun, *"is the customary code of polite behaviour in society or among members of a particular group or profession"*. - So if you are African or Indian, then you do it your way!

Shakespeare wrote *"All the world's a stage, And all the men and women merely players."*

However, *the players* in the production of a wedding are almost without exception rank amateurs acting with no rehearsal in the one-off production of a lifetime. By engaging a director with knowledge of formal etiquette will prevent it from being potentially a very costly flop and ensure it becomes a great success and quite possibly the hit of the decade.

Enjoy

James
The Man in the Red Coat

Contents

Dedication

"To Maddie and Rebecca, Thank you for your understanding and all the tolerance you show me as I disrupt many of our family evenings and weekends, so that I can make a difference to other people's lives."

Chapter One

"What is the point of etiquette?"

Over the following chapters I am going to layout the etiquette and role it plays with both ceremony and individuals at a wedding. The wedding in question is based around a traditional English wedding, but could ultimately apply to any wedding. I will attempt to show what was and what is now relevant.

Subjects to be covered will include photographs, speeches, clothing, the bride, the bridegroom, the parents, the bridal party (including the best man, the head bridesmaid/maid of honour, bridesmaids, ushers, page boys and flower girls etc), the guests, the gift list, the wedding breakfast (including table plan), the cutting of the cake, the departure of the bride and bridegroom, and even the release of doves! So please enjoy the chapters and I hope they are of help, as well as in some cases a bit of an eye opener to both the past, present and may be, even the future.

Etiquette at weddings is something that is gradually being diluted in this "modern" age, and in many cases rightly so. This is mainly because some rituals are no longer relevant in the modern world or that they are no longer even PC!

So I will be looking back at the etiquette of an English wedding, although many things apply to other cultures too, in particular the Hindu and Sikh worlds. If you are a planner or a couple currently in the planning stages, you can check out ideas that you may wish to include, or you may wish not to!

Etiquette, as mentioned in the "foreword", as defined by the Oxford English Dictionary is described as follows: Noun, "is the customary code of polite behaviour in society or among members of a particular group or profession".

Well that sounds like a load of old cobblers doesn't it? Or does it?

I think not. Actually it has often been proven that the most formal of events turn out to be the most relaxed, because either everybody knows their place or they will be given clear instruction as to what it is.

So whilst in some eyes etiquette is seen as elitist and pointless, in fact it provides the structure by which any event, not just a wedding, can be conducted in a relaxed and well informed manor. In modern times this may seem, a bit like using a toastmaster, "why would you want one of them?" But having these guidelines (and a toastmaster) really does make a difference and nowhere more than the Asian wedding world where British formal etiquette is being adopted ever increasingly.

So if you want to know what the rules are please read on in the chapters that follow. I am sure you will find them interesting and help you in the planning of your wedding or any great event, be it yours or anybody else's.

Chapter Two

Weddings of all kinds.

Etiquette, provides a structure by which formalities and things can happen. If the Toastmaster is a visual and audible aid, then the etiquette forms the rules by which we should all ideally adhere.

Most of the following chapters are based around a traditional British, possibly Greek, or even Jewish wedding, which have always tended to have a formal structure to them.

What happens at an Indian, or African Wedding?

Well there is no doubt that these are less structured historically, but the Couples in the UK, no matter where their ancestry heralds from, are very "Westernised" and have reached a compromise between their culture and wanting to achieve so much in an organised fashion.

African weddings like the traditional English ones, tend to follow a clear structure too. Their biggest misunderstanding of etiquette is normally around speeches and their timings. As for Caribbean weddings, these are more relaxed with bigger very cheerful entrances and if I am honest, could benefit with a little more of the structure British etiquette brings!

A large Muslim wedding may have upwards of 800 people. The invites will go out and it will almost encourage a "bring a friend" clause as part of it. Therefore nobody knows quite who is who in some cases. This is highly welcoming, but not always practical. Needless to say there is often spare food available. However, there is so much to see and they are always very friendly.

A large Hindu or Sikh wedding however, even with large numbers, do seem to follow a plan and structure more often. They are also embracing many of the etiquette ideas that we shall be looking at in the following chapters, and clearly benefit from them. I have to admit I really enjoy a good Asian wedding in the UK, because of the rich mixture of embracing both cultural traditions and British etiquette traditions, as well as many of the modern ideas and subtle changes that are clearly relevant to modern society.

And speaking of modern society, where would be without the Rainbow. When the rules of etiquette were first adopted the idea that someone of the same sex could get married was utterly unheard of. In fact it would have been condemnation only. I have always believed in the individual and what is fair. Persecution still exists, but I am glad to say attitudes have changed and we can embrace the fact that everybody in UK society is at last getting a fairer choice in life, or at least it is heading that way.

The thing is, how does etiquette apply in these circumstances? Well, in exactly the same way. Some of the genders of the roles may have been juggled a bit, but once you work out who is who, then the rules still apply. As for your average LGBTQ Wedding, they are always such fun. Trust me if you want to party, get an invite, but whatever you do, please remember to RSVP!

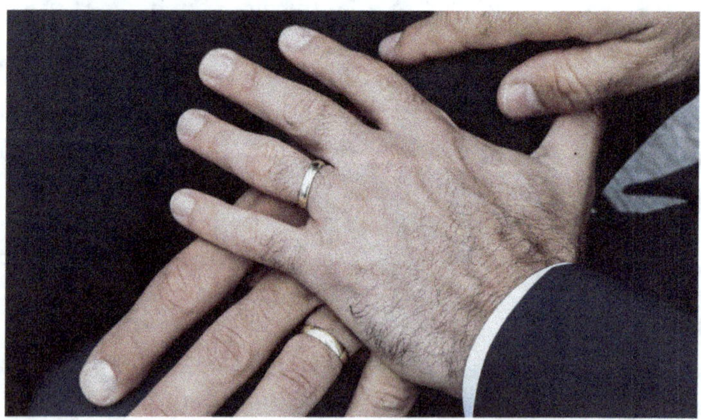

Chapter Three

The Invitation

In the first chapter we considered the point about whether etiquette is elitist or even pointless and as I mentioned, I think not.

So where should the instructions that etiquette provides begin?

They should begin with the invitation. Traditionally the invitation was sent out by the Family of the Bride, however as couples are more involved these days, very often it is the couple who send them out.

On the invite should be the following:

- Who the invite is from. (Either Mr & Mrs Bride, Miss Bride & Mr 'Groom, or in the case of Divorced Parents Mr Bride & Mrs Bride)
- What the invite is for. (Request the pleasure of your company at the marriage of their daughter Miss Bride to Mr 'Groom.)
- Where they are invited to attend. What time they are invited to attend. If it is purely for the marriage or at a reception to follow, or both.
- Who the invite is for exactly. This means if it is a family, the names of children should be included where applicable. Or it could even be Mr, or Miss whoever + Guest

- Where, to whom and by when, the reply should be sent including address, email address and telephone number if applicable. (RSVP)
- What should be worn (If themed – or "Black Tie"). *
- Gift notification if specific instructions needed. *
- Finally, ideally where applicable, protocol dictates that you should always try and address the invite to the woman**. (This is presumably because if you send it to the man, they will probably forget to note it down!)

(*These two are optional only and in fact the last one is often considered "bad form". However, the clarity it brings, tells people what they can give if they wish.)

(**This last one is one that could be dropped. It was considered at the time that the women ran the house and engagements. This may still be the case in your household, but it is no longer politically correct as roles are supposed to be shared more evenly these days (even if in most houses the women still take on the lions share, even if they are also in full time employment).

So whilst this may seem quite a bit to include in/on an invitation it provides very clear guidelines to all and what is expected. Some might think receiving an invitation with all this info' might be a bit overwhelming. Trust me though, it is far less overwhelming than arriving at a wedding at the wrong time, wearing the wrong clothes and carrying an inappropriate gift!

Additionally if your wedding is multicultural it helps to give a clear schedule and or a guide to any ceremonies as this will add to the inclusion and relaxation of "outsiders".

Chapter Four

The Bride

Let us make this quite clear from the outset, a wedding day is all about the bride.

Etiquette dictates that everybody defers to her and her wishes. To give you an example, whenever a Toastmaster makes an announcement his preamble goes "Bride, Bridegroom, Parents of the Bride and Bridegroom, Ladies and Gentlemen". She comes first in everything.

Additionally, if gentlemen are allowed to remove their jackets at the wedding breakfast, it is the bride who gives permission for them to do so. Likewise with ladies fascinators.

Before the wedding, etiquette dictates her role as follows:

- She is instrumental in the organisation
- She is involved with virtually every decision about the day.

Including all the following:
- The Cake
- The Flowers
- The invitations
- The theme of the day (if there is one)
- The wedding dress and shoes
- The headdress – tiara, flowers, veil etc
- The timings on the day

Chapter 4. - The Bride

Including all the following - continued

- The accompanying jewellery
- The Bridesmaids dresses and shoes
- She will suggest to the bridegroom as to how his ushers should be attired
- She will also choose how guests are to be attired
- She will also choose and purchase the Bridegrooms wedding ring if he is to wear one
- She will choose and buy a gift for the Bridegroom as well.

On the day itself she may be fashionably late arriving at the ceremony. (2 to 5 mins is acceptable – anymore is considered bad form.)

She will also receive her Guests with her Husband and their Parents before all head into the wedding breakfast. (This is called a receiving line.)

Once at the wedding breakfast she will sit with her husband sitting to her left. (On her right as the guests looking at her.)

OK, that was what used to happen.

In reality 90% of this is still the case. However, things have become more collaborative between the Bride and Bridegroom than it ever used to be. In my experience it is still the Brides who are the organised ones in each couple, with spreadsheets being under their control! Most Bridegrooms I speak to, have no idea what is actually going on, but they are very happy to agree to the ride.

How am I supposed to pee in this? "Bridesmaids - HELP!!"

As for the receiving line, many don't bother with this ritual, partly because they can take time form an already packed schedule and also the numbers at many weddings these days mean they can take too long. However, I recommend that they are done wherever the schedule permits, because although no conversations are allowed, everybody gets to feel included. If they are not done, then I suggest that the Bride and Bridegroom visit tables during the wedding breakfast whenever possible.

Chapter Five

The Bridegroom

As mentioned in the last chapter, most bridegrooms I work with are almost clueless with regards to their wedding. The Bride has said do it and they have. However, whilst this is very common, there are some who are punching well above their weight and go above and beyond what etiquette actually requires them to do.

So what does etiquette say about the role of the bridegroom?

Before it all gets underway there are a couple questions and a certain item of jewellery to get sorted.

First, before even asking his Bride, he should seek the approval of his prospective Father-in-law by asking for the hand of his daughter in marriage. Assuming that approval is granted, he must then procure an engagement ring and then if the first question didn't cause him enough in the way of nerves and stress, he must pop the question to his beloved.

Now that the engagement is on and the Bride is busy planning the wedding he does have one of two things he needs to arrange himself.

Chapter 5. - The Bridegroom

He has joint responsibility with the Bride over choosing the wedding venue and photographer. He must also, with help from his parents create the Bridegroom's family guest list. This he should then present to the Bride's Mother for processing. While the Bride needs to work out with her Father how to get to the ceremony and reception, the Bridegroom is obviously responsible for how he gets there too. However and more importantly he is responsible for sorting the "going away" transport for himself and his Bride. This may or may not be a surprise to the Bride. (The transport, and hopefully not that he has done it!)

On the day itself he should arrive at the ceremony space at least 20 (ideally 40) minutes prior to it taking place. Once the register is signed and they are officially Husband and Wife he should walk his Wife down the aisle with her on his left (leaving his right arm – his sword arm, available to draw his sword should he need to protect her!). Once at the venue, like and with his Bride he will form part of a receiving line to greet Guests.

Following the speech by the Father of the Bride, the Bridegroom will respond to the speech, by first thanking him on behalf of him and his new wife for the toast he has just proposed and then he would thank his Parents-in-law for allowing him to marry her. He would also thank everybody involved with the production of the wedding finishing by thanking the Bridal Party, after which he will propose a toast to them.

Once the speeches are concluded the cake is to be cut and here he will let his Wife hold the knife but he will wrap his hands around hers, "giving her guidance".

Chapter 5. - The Bridegroom

Then it is time to dance. Traditionally he would have initially asked his Mother-in-law to dance first. During the dance his Father-in-law would "cut in" leaving him free to lead his Wife onto the dancefloor for their "first dance".……. and relax.

In reality, like the Bride in chapter four, 90% of this is still done. **The biggest changes** in this modern world being, the frequently dropped receiving line, and in particular the dance order. This is normally done as follows in this day and age.

1st Dance - Bride and Bridegroom
2nd Dance - Bride and Father, with Bridegroom and his Mother joining a little into the dance and then Mother of the Bride and Father of the Bridegroom a little further after.
3rd Dance - The rest of the world!

Party on.

"Here you go my dear - Honeymoon beckons"

Chapter Six

The Parents of the Bride and Bridegroom

Well let us be blindingly obvious here, but without these two couples the Bride and Bridegroom would not exist and there would be no wedding at all. However, who is the most important and why?

In the world of Husbands there is the time honoured joke about the Mother-in-law. I am very lucky I have had the most wonderful Mother-in-laws, as I am sure most men in my position have too.

It is however, the Mother of the Bride who is considered top person. "Wonder Woman" if you like, but she is to be closely supported by her Husband, normally with his cheque book or his ability to make bank transfers as is the case these days.

His financial responsibilities are traditionally as follows. He pays for:

- Order of service sheets.
- Announcements in local press.
- The cake.
- Bride's dress.
- Bridesmaids' dresses.
- Reception venue hire.
- Catering at the reception.
- Entertainment and decorations at the reception.
- Bride's transport to and from the wedding ceremony.

Chapter 6. - The Parents of the Bride and Bridegroom

Bride Father's Financial Responsibilities - Continued

- Church or Ceremony flowers.
- Flowers at the reception.
- Photographer/Videographer.
- and most importantly of all the Toastmaster!

Before the day, both the Bride's parents have much to do. Starting with the engagement party, which they should arrange and host. They will also support the Bride and Bridegroom with their choice of venue.

So back to Wonder Woman. The Mother of the Bride traditionally not only creates the guest list for her family, she is to approve the one passed to her by the Bridegroom.

She is the Man Friday to the Bride's Robinson Crusoe. She is there to help, to guide, to support the Bride in all her decisions, as well as on the day. However, and this is the most important thing. She is to act as counsel, without necessarily forcing her own ideas upon her Daughter. She has to remember to respect her Daughter's wishes, even if, *and I want to make this quite clear,* they are not aligned with her own.

Invariably the Mother of the Bride is also in charge of the catering, cake and flowers.

As for Father of the Bride his responsibilities go some way further than his financial contribution. That tends to be before the wedding, but on the wedding day itself he is the busiest of the parents, or at least with regards to allocated roles.

- He will accompany his Daughter to the ceremony and lead her up the aisle.
- He will "give her away"
- He like his Wife is likely to witness the signing of the register.
- He will then accompany the Bridegroom's mother back down the aisle on the exit of the ceremony.
- He will be actively meeting guests at the reception
- He will receive the guests with the Bride and Bridegroom, his Wife and the Bridegroom's parents.

- He will make the first speech proposing the toast to the Bride and Bridegroom.
- He will at some point dance with his Daughter
- He is traditionally the last to leave the venue after he bids farewell to the Guests.

So with all this being done by the Bride's parents, what is there to do for the Bridegroom's?

Well frankly, not a lot. They must remember to congratulate the Parents of the Bride after the announcement of the engagement. At that point they should also instigate a meeting between them with respect to any arrangements, but frankly they are only for approval. They play no official part in their creation

On the day they must turn up looking smart, probably witness the signing of the register, be part of the receiving line if there is one and be prepared to dance. They will be on the top table, so they need to behave too!

That was the theory. This is the more likely modern day reality.

The Bride's Mother will do her bit as described, hopefully respecting her Daughter's wishes. Dad will do his bit, although he may not be the last to leave the reception these days. He may also no longer be the one forking out for everything.

Chapter 6. - The Parents of the Bride and Bridegroom

Also as many people wish to propose the toast to the bride and bridegroom he should more likely propose the toast to his "daughter only", as she is the one he has been talking about in his speech.

As for the Bridegroom's parents they are likely to be more involved than they ever used to be. Financially and probably in the whole planning of things indicates that their role has definitely increased over the years.

Finally, more and more often the Parents of the Bride and Bridegroom are no longer displayed on the top table. This is partly to do with sadly so many broken marriages, but also to do with the choice of the couple.

"Dad, if you could just look this way please - especially as you have paid for it"!

Chapter Seven

The Best Man

So let us begin before the wedding. Etiquette dictates that it is the Best Man who has to arrange the Stag Party. This should not be the night before as it is always done in the movies for comedic effect. Normally the previous weekend or even a month before where neither work nor the wedding can be disturbed by high jinks.

Then on the day the list is seemingly endless.

- The first and most crucial role is to get the Bridegroom to the ceremony early and most importantly sober.
- He should bring with him the ring(s)
- Then if he is sensible he is to organise the Ushers. He can delegate the following;*

1. Fitting of button holes
2. Issuing the order of service
3. Organising the seating within the ceremony
4. Organising the collection of wedding presents and storing them safely
5. Organising that the Bride and Bridegroom's luggage to go away, is in the right place

Chapter 7. - The Best Man

- He should arrange payment of the Clergyman.
- He should be beside the Bridegroom for support and to handover the rings at the right time.
- He should witness the signing of the register
- He should accompany the Head Bridesmaid up the aisle at the end of the ceremony
- He should make a speech in response to the toast to the bridesmaids/bridal party
- He should read out any messages or telegrams from absent friends and family
- He should share the first dance with the Head Bridesmaid
- He should check that everybody is having a good time.
- When it is all over he should return any hired clothing with Head Bridesmaid to the outfitters.

Not much then. That is why so many people accept being Best Man with reluctance. It is not just about the speech, but that can be the biggest hindrance of all.

So what has changed?

In principal most of the above still stands if no Toastmaster is engaged. If a Toastmaster is engaged he can take charge of all the administrative type roles. All the delegated jobs that are given to the ushers are passed to him to either carry out or delegate (again to the ushers who need something to do!).

As for telegrams these were replaced by faxes 25 years ago and these were in turn superseded by emails or even WhatsApps! These can be also passed to the Toastmaster.

Finally at the end of his speech. If the toast given by the Father of the Bride is only to his daughter, then the Best Man gets to give the Toast to the Bride and Bridegroom but only if there is to be a further response. This is very common now as invariably Brides get to say a few words.

Anyway, regardless of how much he has to do, or she as is often the case, they generally need a week off after it all! It is definitely the shared most difficult role on the day – that is unless you employ a Toastmaster.

Chapter Eight

The Head Bridesmaid or Maid of Honour

Having now learned about the responsibilities of the Best Man, the Head Bridesmaid or Maid of Honour (If married already) has much the same role for the Bride as he has for the Bridegroom.

She will begin with helping the bride choose her wedding dress (and by advising her what she is also prepared to be seen in!). She will then be instrumental in arranging the Hen night!

Additionally before the day, as the invitations have come from the Bride's family she is to assist the Bride and her mother with recording the accepted and declined invitations.

Her main responsibility on the day is to continue to support to the Bride, and there are no shortage of jobs for her to keep her eye on. If anything she is even busier than the Best Man, although she officially does not have the responsibility of making a speech.

So following is a list of just some of what she is supposed to be doing.

- She will help the Bride with getting ready and with any changes of clothes throughout the day.

- She will be confirming final details with the photographer and wedding car, as well as florist, venue and caterer or she will speak to the Toastmaster who she can delegate some of these tasks to.
- At the church or ceremony venue she will greet the bride outside to check that the dress is settled as it should be once the bride has stepped out of any transport. She will check the Bride's Father too. She will also be doing this for the Bride throughout the day.
- While the Best Man is organising the Ushers/Groomsmen, she will be organising the other Bridesmaids, Flower Girls and Page Boys.
- During the ceremony when the Best Man is looking after the rings the Head Bridesmaid is holding the Bride's bouquet.
- She will also be one of the witnesses of the signing of the register.
- After the ceremony she will be making sure that the Bride's change of clothes if required is ready and she will have already checked that the Bride has everything ready to take with her on her honeymoon.
- At the reception she will assist the Best Man in guiding people and introducing guests to each other, unless there is a Toastmaster present.
- Finally she will along with the Best Man return any hired clothing to outfitters as well as save a piece of Wedding Cake until the couple return from their honeymoon.

Basically, she is everything to the Bride and if the Bride's Mother was Wonder Woman, the Head Bridesmaid is Super Girl. Available at the Bride's beck and call at any time of day or night leading up to the wedding and a complete dogsbody on the day including those involuntary trips to the loo! Some Brides think about this last task when choosing a dress, others do not. Enough said!

Chapter 8. - The Head Bridesmaid or Maid of Honour
So who wants the job?!

Well, that was the official line. What happens today is slightly less fraught.

She is still the Bride's PA, on duty in a pretty full-on fashion, but much of what she is responsible for in the above is now highly "transferable". These days most bridal couples do not drive away at the end of the wedding reception but stay the night in a honeymoon suite at the venue. They often breakfast the following day with family and friends before departing. Therefore things tend to be less stressful than they used to be.

The point is, as long as the Bride has created a proper schedule there is no need to panic, but if you take on the roll, make sure that she has done so, or you will end up frazzled.

Additionally if the Bride has engaged a Toastmaster or Planner, they take on around 75% of the old tasks Etiquette used to insist the Head Bridesmaid did. Hopefully they have and then the Head Bridesmaid should have a brilliant day too.

Chapter Nine

The Bridal Party

This could also be titled – "aka anyone else who has a job to do but is not the Bride, Bridegroom, Parents of the Bride and Bridegroom, Best Man and Head Bridesmaid!"

Generally included in this are; Groomsmen, Ushers, Bridesmaids, Flower Girls and Page Boys.

First, let's look at the difference between a Groomsman and an Usher.

Groomsmen are normally, or historically, closer to the couple, either by family or very close friends. Whereas Ushers, may have been employed or may not be quite so close to the couple and may have even missed out on some of the pre-wedding events – or at least they may have done in the past. However, on the day they are fundamentally the same and sometimes the difference in the role is only the names they have been given!

On the day they are the Best Man and Bride Groom's "Posse", for want of a better phrase and invariably they don't have to work too hard. However, a good one is worth his weight in gold and can really help remove some of the stress from the "Dynamic Duo".

Their main role is normally at ceremony time. Under the guidance of the Best Man (or Toastmaster if present) they are to help get people sat down in the right place. Traditionally in Church or registry weddings, they greet guests at the door with an order of service and then walk them to their seats.

Additionally, they should carry out anything else that is instructed by the Best Man or Bridegroom, as was mentioned in Chapter 7, The Best Man.

In the same way that the Ushers assist the men, the Bridesmaids assist the women, taking direction from the Head Bridesmaid/Maid of Honour and the Bride. They must look fabulous, but be careful not to be too fabulous as they should not ideally overshadow the Bride.

As for the Page Boys. They are to provide a bit of the wow factor to the bridal procession. They invariably take on the role of Ring Bearer if present.

Finally, we have the Flower Girls. These are "Bridesmaids in the making" and lead the Bridal Party down the aisle. Their job is to shower the ground ahead of the Bride with soft freshly picked petals for her to walk on. The role also includes looking "cute" along with the Page Boys, bringing a wonderful ahhhh factor to the procession.

So what has changed over recent decades?

The biggest has to be the interchanging of gender between the roles. Whilst the Flower Girls and Page Boys have not changed the gender, the role they do has become swapped quite often.

As for the Bridesmaids and Ushers (less so if they are Groomsmen) these too have become much more flexible with everybody swapping roles. The Ushers still perform their role but it is not uncommon to find a female Usher. Likewise, whilst not necessarily a male Bridesmaid, a Man of Honour can often be spotted in the Brides entourage.

What does make a big difference to this extension of the Bridal Party, is using a Toastmaster and or Wedding Coordinator. They can make these roles much more relaxing on the day allowing those in the roles to know that they are going to be guided and not have to think when it is their turn to do things and how they are to be done. That means they get to enjoy the day too.

Chapter Ten

The Guests

Make no mistake here, as a Guest, there is a way to do things at a traditional wedding, that follow a certain amount of etiquette and protocol.

The first thing a Guest must do is reply formally to the invitation. You must let the Family know that you are coming. Food, when it is provided, forms quite a bit of any wedding budget and it is bad form, even if you are not going, to not reply because the caterers need to know how many are coming.

Then there is the gift. Ideally chosen from a wedding gift list. You can if you are clever, go for one of the larger items that individuals may struggle to afford, by joining with others that are going and all chipping in to make up the amount needed to purchase said item.

The next most important thing is to arrive where instructed punctually. Even a little early to avoid rushing at the last minute. It is OK for the Bride to keep you waiting a few minutes, but not the other way around.

If children are present, then it is the parents' responsibility to make sure that they are under control and well looked after. It is not fair on the Bride and Bridegroom to have children running riot or making a noise during crucial parts of any ceremony or having them upstage the couple with their antics. **Ahhhh is one thing, Arrrrrrgh is another!**

Chapter 10. - The Guests

It is important that when a Guest meets either set of Parents and or the Bride and Bridegroom that they remember to thank them for their kind invitation. If a Receiving Line is being run this is the one thing along with congratulations that should be said as you pass down the line. (More about that in Chapter 11.)

Guests should listen to instructions given by any of the bridal party, a Wedding Coordinator or if present a Toastmaster/MC, and follow them swiftly. This follows the issue of being punctual. If asked to go and take seats at the wedding breakfast, it is important that they go immediately rather than hang around chatting and thinking they will go when they are ready. There will be a schedule of events and by adding to lateness can cause real problems, especially with the service of food. **Remember as a Guest it is not your day, it is theirs.**

Gentlemen should keep their jackets on, even at table, and ladies should keep their hats and fascinators in place. That is unless the Bride gives them permission to remove them!

Confetti should be thrown only when and where instructed.

Finally, it is not thought good form to heckle during the speeches. One should listen and only react when encouraged!

So that is what used to be important. But what is important today? ....Well actually it all still applies. You should follow instructions given and if you do, everybody will have a wonderful day.

As for removing jackets and fascinators, it is amazing how many people think they should just walk into the wedding breakfast and remove them! It makes for a bit of fun when as a Toastmaster I get to announce "..... And gentlemen, for those of you who have not already removed your jackets, you NOW have the Brides permission to do so!" It normally gets a chuckle from partners and the occasional elbow in the ribs for offenders.

Chapter Eleven

The Wedding Breakfast and the before and after.

Culturally there are going to be big differences here for all of the following, but what follows is a basis that could work at any wedding breakfast (or dinner) that has a seating plan.

So let's begin with the seating plan itself. How these are created are totally up to the choice of the couple. However, there things to remember.

- Historically the top table would include the Couple, the Parents, the Best Man and the Head Bridesmaid.

- As you look at it – Bridesmaid, Father of 'Groom, Mother of Bride, Bridegroom, Bride, Father of Bride, Mother of 'Groom, Best Man.

- Then you build out from the top table in order of importance. So the tables nearest have the direct relatives with friends being further away.

- If numbers are under 150 then a straight plan with table numbers and names is sufficient.

- If more than 150 then an alphabetical list with table name/number stated after name, with a separate plan showing the room in map form.

- All should be on clear backing with bold block writing. Italics look wonderful but in practicality they are difficult to read.

Nowadays you can set the tables as you like. As long as the plan is clear, that is the most important thing.

Chapter 11. - The Wedding Breakfast - Before and After

Now that everybody has viewed the table plan they need to be called to take their seats. If a Receiving Line has not be done as the guests initially arrived (as is often the case as it is not always practical) then now is the other time to do it, if one is to be held.

What is a Receiving Line? It is a way that all the guests get to formally say hello to the Bride and Bridegroom and their parents.

Who should be in the Receiving Line? Basically the top table as mentioned before. However, the Best Man and Maid of Honour are optional as they may be attending to other duties. What happens at a Receiving Line? Each Guest gives their name to the Toastmaster/MC, who will call their name out loud enough so that all within the Receiving Line can hear it. They proceed to the first person in line (the Father of the Bride), say hello, shake hands or peck on the cheek if appropriate and then move on to the next person (the Mother of the Bride). This is repeated with the whole line and then the Guest goes into the Wedding Breakfast to find their seat.

The rules state no conversation is to be entered into. You should also present your invitation to the Toastmaster or Master of Ceremonies.

Nowadays many do not bother with a receiving line. Obviously this is not practical at a wedding of upward of 150 people. This I think is a shame, as having one means everybody gets seen by the Bride and Bridegroom. Also the addition of a "high five" has been added to the list of things that it is appropriate to do. Finally, whatever name you give to the Toastmaster/MC, is the name they will call out. There's always one who wants to be "Mickey Mouse"! It can be a lot of fun though. Needless to say nobody ever remembers their invitation these days!

So everyone has made their way through the Receiving Line and they have found their place at table. We now have to get the line itself into the room. For the Parents this can be done in one of two ways. They can subtly make their way to table or they can be formally announced into the room. I prefer the latter as it shows their place and allows them their 5 seconds of fame.

Once the Parents are "installed" it is time to get the Bride and Bridegroom in. The room should be standing as they come in and make their way to the top table. If a Toastmaster is present he should have briefed the room as to what is to happen.

Chapter 11. - The Wedding Breakfast - Before and After

If a grace is to be said it will be done before all take their seats. However, grace or not, the Bride must be sat first. Once she is seated all the rest are invited to take theirs also. This is likely to be the point that the Bride may decide to grant permission for the Men to remove their jackets and for the Women who have them, to remove their hats or fascinators.

Food service commences and at the end of desert speeches are held. If there is a coffee course and the Loyal Toast to Her Majesty the Queen is being proposed then this would happen between desert clearance and coffee. (Before the speeches)

Once all are completed then it will be time to cut the cake, followed by dancing and revelry.

How is the cake cut? Being flippant, with a knife! However, etiquette states that it is the Bride who always holds the knife, but as mentioned in chapter 6 her husband wraps his hands around hers "for guidance". (How wonderfully patronising!)

What happens these days is a grace is being said less and less. However, I regularly read a non-secular one that I will have created and is relevant to the day. They are designed to make people smile, rather than be repentant, but also to make people think of others less fortunate than themselves, whilst at the same acknowledging a blessing on the occasion.

Toasts to the Sovereign are now very rare, except at Jewish Weddings where loyalty to our Sovereign and to the President of the State of Israel are always observed with a loyal toast to each. (Separately of course.)

Speeches also seem to move around quite a bit. They sometimes take place at the very beginning of the meal and or even between courses. Additionally it is also quite common these days for couples to cut the cake as soon as they enter the Wedding Breakfast before going to take a seat. This last note is very popular in Indian culture.

Does any of this matter? Well some of the behavioural items should really be observed or at least acknowledged. As for the running order? No, with the exception of a loyal toast if one is to be given, none of it is vital as long as the schedule is clear.

Chapter Twelve

"My Ceremony and Other Animals!"

In this chapter, we are going to touch base on some of the things that also happen at a wedding. These are in some cases vital while others form part of the dressing.

So let us begin with photographs.

Almost without exception there is a photographer at every wedding to capture the occasion. This can be a solitary relative at a quiet affair, or it can be your "Bollywood Exclusive" full on production team of about four capturing every move and they are supported by a video team of a similar number.

The number of photographers is irrelevant. They are there to do a job and get the photos the Couple require. Etiquette in this field though has recently taken on some seriously heavy modification. Why? Social Media and the introduction of the Smart Phone.

Etiquette in the past was all about group photographs. Who should be in each etc. These are still very important. They are important because they are the snapshot in time into a family history. These are the shots that come up on "who do you think you are?" Oh look, it's Auntie

Chapter 12. - My Ceremony and Other Animals

Jane and that was Uncle Bob - He still had his beard then!

So where does the new etiquette fit in? Two things immediately jump to mind : Because there is an official team taking pictures, nobody else has to. So put your phone away. However, if the Couple does not wish everybody taking pictures of the day they should make a formal announcement about their wishes. They should also make the professionally taken photos available to all at a later date. Additionally if you have professional photographers, they should not have to fight their way through relatives to get to the shot.

So often video footage ends up on the cutting room floor because it is spoiled by people with their phones out. Just imagine, "here comes the Bride". She is walking serenely up the aisle with her father being filmed from both ends of the room. She looks so happy and as the video pulls back from her face to reveal the room with all her family and friends present and her husband to be, waiting expectantly, all we see is a wall of camera phones filming it too. Nobody is in the moment, they just want a picture! This is very sad. Sometimes it is made even worse by the "uncle" who has travelled from afar with his big lens camera who actually is stepping onto the aisle to get his best shots to take home to others.

Then we have the problem of social media. If you wish to take a picture of yourself and may be some friends "at the wedding of....", then that is fine. Post it immediately. Tell everybody that you are having a great time. But posting a live video of your friend coming down the aisle is beyond out of order. Unless they have given you express permission to do this, it is not fair. So don't do it. Most of the weddings I now work at, we put a 48-hour ban on pictures other than selfies being posted on social media and rightly so. Let the couple choose what they wish posted. It is their day, not yours.

Chapter 12. - My Ceremony and Other Animals

Tossing of the bouquet. - So she is about to leave, to go away with her new husband off to her new life. She has patiently held onto that beautiful bouquet of flowers all day and it has served its purpose. So what does she do? Throw it away, but not in a bin, but to whom she thinks is the most worthy contender to get married next.

It seems we have come full circle on this, well almost. Originally the Bride would have looked to whom she was throwing the flowers and she could have thrown it to either a male or female recipient. However, then it became a bun fight with screaming women all jostling for place as the Bride launches the bouquet over her shoulder into the scrum behind her. (Such decorum!)

Nowadays we have a mixture of the two, where men are once again standing as expectant recipients. Depending on whether you are in Mayfair, Devon or dare I say it Essex, the level of noise and expectation and behaviour varies considerably. However, no one can deny it isn't a wonderful bit of fun!

So where were we? Oh yes the Bride was about to leave and go off on her honeymoon with her husband. Traditionally after the cake cutting and a little bit of dancing it would time for the married couple to make their departure. This would be in the transportation arranged by the husband. It could be anything. In some cultures, this can take some time as certain fines need to be paid and nuts need to be broken!

In western cultures, this is normally a highly joyous sending off. Mums cry a bit, but for everyone else, it is normally fun especially if the transport is being given a makeover! However, in other cultures, this really is the big goodbye and can be very emotionally charged for all concerned – almost funeral-like in some cases.

Chapter 12. - *My Ceremony and Other Animals*

So hopefully the Bridegroom has sorted the "wheels" appropriately, preferably with a chauffeur and they can depart into the evening, off to spend their first night together alone!

Nowadays, more often than not, and depending on the venue, the Bride and Bridegroom don't leave at all. They party into the night collapsing in the "honeymoon suite" in the early hours. The following morning they get up and have breakfast with friends and family before possibly heading home, or to the airport to catch that flight to their dream destination.

Reasons behind this include; stricter drink-drive limits, the bride and bridegroom have already spent the night together, logistics-wise it is much easier meaning the party can go on longer and the Couple get to spend more time with their family and friends.

The downside is the Couple get to see the aftermath of the party, not always a good thing, although sometimes hilarious. It also means that the aforementioned bouquet tossing now needs to be scheduled rather than at a natural departing point. However, these are minor things to consider.

From an etiquette point of view however, there is nothing to say how this is done and therefore – freestyle and do what you like.

Chapter Thirteen

"Ideas beyond etiquette - hints and tips, just for fun"

In this penultimate chapter, I offer you a checklist of most of the things to remember and suggestions and ideas of things you could include as part of your day.

It is less about what you should do and more about what you may or could do.

Some will cost money and others will not, other than perhaps a little time.

So let us begin with your checklist for the day.

- How big an event? - Schedule
- Date(s)
- Planner (if you need one)
- Venue (Country House / Hotel / Barn / Marquee / Garden / Beach /Virtual)
- Bridal Party
- Dress(es) and Uniform(s)
- Caterer (if not venue)
- Decor (if not venue)
- Entertainment (Band/DJ)
- Photographer
- Videographer
- Church/Synagogue/Gurdwara
- Priest/Pandit/Imam/Rabbi
- Cake
- Flowers
- Dancefloor (if not venue)
- Rings
- Invitations
- Transport
- Favours
- Hair and Make Up
- Table Plan
- TOASTMASTER or MC

Chapter 13. - Ideas Beyond Etiquette

Now that you have your list you will need to interview each of your suppliers. My recommendation is that you interview at least three of each type, even if you still go for the first one.

This is especially important with planners, photographers, hair and make up, and toastmaster or mc. The reason is, these are the people you are going to spend the most one to one time with throughout the day(s). Photographers may take great photos and the toastmaster may be a terrific speaker, but you really have to get on with them as well. If you don't they will wind you up and you just do not want that on this day of all days.

So now we come to some great ideas that can really make a difference;

- Have a theme and up to a point encourage others to be a part of it. (I have worked at themed events as Dumbledore from Harry Potter, Lumiere from Beauty and the Beast as well as Qui Con Gin from Star Wars Episode 1 (for a wedding held on May the 4th no less!).
- Photobooths/mirrors are always popular and help capture peoples real sense of fun and humour.
- An extra individual family group shot photographer. Everyone is generally dressed up at a wedding. Therefore, why not have someone doing group shots that can be kept with everyone looking their best.
- Additional entertainers
    o A magician (close up going around tables)
    o A caricaturist or cartoonist (kept forever)
    o A silhouettist (much cooler than caricaturist)
    o A RAP artist!
    o Dohl Players
    o A dance act
    o A children's entertainer/creche
    o A musical act of some kind - violinist or singing waiters
    o A Casino
    o A Flash Mob!
- Transport - 3 Types to consider Bride/Bridesmaids arrival (unseen by most), 'Groom Arrival (Depending on culture this can be a massive viewing point) and the going away.
    o Bride/Bridesmaids - needs lots of space
        ▪ Limousine - new or classic
        ▪ Horse and Carriage

- Transport continued
  - Groom (two seats only necessary)
    - Helicopter! (Depends on your venue)
    - Supercar - followed by your posse in theirs
    - A classic car
    - A Tuk-Tuk or Rickshaw
    - A horse
    - Nothing special just walk in with your groomsmen like in "Reservoir dogs"
    - A mechanical elephant
  - Going away (two seats only necessary, or a chauffeur)
    - Your own car
    - A taxi
    - a chauffeur driven car or any kind
    - Any of the above with the exception of the Horse, Elephant. Tuk-Tuk and Posse!
  - Guests
    - Coach, Minibus or if in London - Routemaster Bus
- Cake ideas
  - Traditional wedding style tiered cake
  - A show cake with a cutting point only and another already pre-cut to use as desert
  - A themed cake - anything from chocolate logs to a Disney cake
  - A naked cake
  - Cupcakes
  - Or a combination of cake and cupcakes. The best example I have seen was of a giant peacock (illustrated below right)
- Fireworks

Finally on a note of caution, one thing to possibly avoid is a comedian. One of the things that makes the human race so fascinating is our variety. However, that also includes our sense of humour. What you may find hilarious, others may struggle to raise a smile to.

Chapter Fourteen

Virtual Wedding Etiquette

Who would have thought at the beginning of 2020 we would even be discussing this subject, but as I write this during the second half of the year we are still locked in the grips of a global pandemic, the likes of which we have not seen for 100 years.

The first question we should ask is, "is there any etiquette surrounding virtual weddings?" Surely being something so new, there cannot be?

This is a great question but given the current situation we find ourselves in we are in unchartered territory, both from running successful weddings in the virtual space, as well as any use of etiquette.

As mentioned in the foreward and chapter One, etiquette as defined by the Oxford English dictionary is, "the customary code of polite behaviour in society or among members of a particular group or profession". – So whatever is done it needs to try and match everybody's way of doing things, and that means in a sensible and correct manner.

Using the guides given in the earlier chapters where we discussed everybody's roles at a wedding, regardless of virtual or not, ideally the modern adapted versions of the etiquette for each should remain and be adhered to wherever possible.

Chapter 14. - Virtual Wedding Etiquette

However, we then come to how does one behave at a virtual wedding?

This will depend on which side of the camera you are on as well as which side of the screen!

Roles as mentioned before should remain much the same and from a hosting point of view, following any schedule you created and broadcasted to your invitees. (Yes the bride can be 2 minutes late!!)

The trick to controlling etiquette has to be a central facilitator who can guide everyone.

The rules from the bridal party's side.

- Confirm a firm schedule – with plenty of breaks or ways for viewers to engage
- Try to keep it as close to being an "in person" celebration
- Send out a wedding pack, including service sheets (for the ceremonial part), and accessories to make everyone feel more a part of the day - even food if you wish.
- Acknowledgement of guests wherever they may be.

The rules from the guest's side.

- RSVP – very important if you want the link and any pack that is to be sent out by the couple.
- Turn up or switch on on time
- Dress appropriately
- Try and stay engaged, because if you are called upon, you need to be able to react.
- Be as much of a part of the day as possible as if you were there in person.
- Applaud, cheer, stand up and sit down at the correct times
- Be ready to have your "screenshot" taken!
- Follow the instructions of the Toastmaster/Host/MC if there is one.
- Leave a message either in the Chat or even better in the form of a video message for the Couple

Chapter 14. - Virtual Wedding Etiquette

It is all about making the celebration work as best for everybody so the etiquette involved is to be a part of it as much as possible. As a couple you have to be clear and reasonable and as a guest it is your role to be really be as engaged and involved as much as you can, really entering into the spirit of the occasion.

Whilst there are no strict rules of etiquette yet for virtual weddings, I hope this gives you food for thought as to the possible. Having run a couple now if you get the planning right they really can be a lot of fun and having run them on Zoom using breakout rooms and microwavable meals sent out, whilst there was no substitute for actually being in the room, they were still a lot of fun in a different way.

Epilogue

So in summation, etiquette is still as relevant today as it was 150 years ago. Yes it may have been modified and adapted, but the fact remains it is still the backbone to any structure that forms a wedding. If we all do our little bit, then days run smoother. Knowledge is power as they say and because etiquette allows us to know our place and our role, it also means relaxation. If you know what you have to do, that is half the battle. If you don't, then anxiety can possibly kick in, and that would be a shame as everybody at a wedding is supposed to have fun and enjoy themselves, after all, it is a celebration.

I have mentioned being able to relax and there is of course that extra thing you can do. You will have noticed a common theme at the end of most of the chapters. By using a wedding planner/coordinator, or in particular on the day a Toastmaster/MC, you let them do all the worrying about the schedules and etiquette. This may be your one and only wedding. You are, as I mentioned in the foreword, the amateurs having to give a one-off performance of a lifetime. As a Toastmaster, I get married about 100 times every 30 months. That brings with it experience and knowledge. Now very few are as busy as I am, but use a toastmaster's ability and skill to guide everybody through your day. This will allow everyone, including you the couple, to relax and really enjoy the celebration that they are a part of and a witness to. It's your party and your choice. Use the etiquette mentioned in this publication to guide you and even help with ideas. However, if you wish to relax as much as your guests too, then get a Man in a Red Coat or even dare I say it, if I am available, *The Man in the Red Coat.* I say Man, but good Women are available too. There is something else etiquette has thankfully adapted to as well.

As for the releasing of Doves that I mentioned in the first chapter. There is no formal etiquette involving them, but they are great fun to watch fly.

As mentioned in Chapter 13 He is not always just
The Man in the Red Coat
Here he is as Albus Percival Wulfric Brian Dumbledore
Pictured in the Great Hall of Hogwarts School of Witchcraft and Wizardry.
(Warner Brothers Studio Tour London - The Making of Harry Potter)